BEING BEYOND RECONFIGURATION

poems by DRU WATKINS

Transcendent Zero Press

Houston, Texas

ISBN-13: 978-1-946460-27-1

Printed in the United States of America

Transcendent Zero Press
16429 El Camino Real Apt. #7
Houston, TX 77062

FIRST EDITION

BEING BEYOND RECONFIGURATION

poems by DRU WATKINS

"…that man is the intermediary between creatures, that he is the familiar of the gods above him as he is the lord of the beings beneath him; that, by the acuteness of his senses, the inquiry of his reason and the light of his intelligence, he is the interpreter of nature, set midway between the timeless unchanging and the flux of time; the living union (as the Persians say), the very marriage hymn of the world, and, by David's testimony but little lower than the angels."

- Giovanni Pico della Mirandola, from *Oration on the Dignity of Man* (1486)

I

Draw a Map

Include mudslides and gallows.
Melted wax marks the oceans.
Menstrual blood from capsized lovers
molds blotched red mountain borders.

Streams of adopted memories.
Latitude spun lengthwise.
Longitude spears the heart
of a restless native.

A call for incessant action.
Trade route veins
pulsate with cinnamon
and salt
to preserve an image
not yet fit to grasp.

Buoyancy

I wear your lapsed sunset like a cataract on my necklace.
We talk for hours as you split my shadow with knotted string.

We compare families like
tree limbs in a trash heap.

Across the swamp and above the fog,
jet black hair.
Curls like a crosshatched question mark.

We both feel a subtle rupture.
Two bodies tumble into the same mind.

It takes a while for the penny to hit the bottom of the well.
The reverberation pings against my spine like a wayward vibrato.
Two half grins equal a missed glance.

I am Europa's bull,
you are the arrow through my muse.
Let us float toward an oceanic equilibrium
until the crags cleave us into separate continents.

Nightlife Fraudster

sits by himself in a bar
penning nonsense.
Words germinate
in a nowhere field.
Couples and carousers
talk over a loud AC.

Like a well-adjusted lobotomy,
he walks into oncoming traffic.
Cars ricochet like marbles.
Self-contained globes
fracture each other
and hide in shag carpet.

He rocks on the barstool.
A hungry infant
falls with his bottle.

Beginning of Music

Wind is the primary instrument.
Breath fuels hands that pound stretched elephant skin
and nebulous notes from a bone flute.

Primeval cries through vocal chords evolve
into melody and rest in language.

Through recycled animal remains,
the human becomes instrumental.

The next super species shall make flutes and drums
from our corpses.
Cosmic triggers in the future of dance.

Pull others into the trance of collective identity.
Wind fills the billows of pulse and rhythm.
The tired heart syncopates with footsteps and nervous twitches.

Dried sheep guts harden in the sun and vibrate in unison
tuned like lutes in tempestuous pregnancies.

Divine Oscillations
reanimate dead matter with time and tone.

Music is predicated on the dead.
Without this inevitable blood sacrifice,
the rhythms of culture would have no cadence.

Promethean Adam

Blessed are the exalted criminals
who escape "God's" skinner box
and catapult history into a
new epoch.

Hallowed transgressors.
Necessary injustice.
Survival of the species
depends on theft.

Political order is the prize.
Man is made to be modified-
an amalgamation of religion,
art, and cunning.

"Zeus" ex machina but Adam confounds the beast.

Part Time Ascetic

When sensual excess
floats to the top
of his consciousness
like a school of bloated trout,
the libertine recoils
as he spits his sip of overindulgence.

We dine at debauchery's marble table.
Belches, opiatic sighs,
and toppled goblets clatter
like jagged peppers in a spice jar.

In a declaration of revolutionary voluptuousness,
the belly usurps the brain
and dons a crown of entrails.

Swirling amnesiac fog
seduces thrill-seekers.
Vaporous chains are choke collars for addicts.

Pleasure grabs the reigns of willpower until
eyes glaze from nausea's panoramic confusion.

Retreat into an empty room with beige walls.
Breathe until boredom sways the appetite to kneel
and listen to the diastolic space of time.

LEADER OF THE CHORUS

Oh, mortal, you who desire to instruct yourself in our great wisdom, the Athenians, the Greeks will envy you your good fortune. Only you must have the memory and ardour for study, you must know how to stand the tests, hold your own, go forward without feeling fatigue, caring but little for food, abstaining from wine, gymnastic exercises and other similar follies, in fact, you must believe as every man of intellect should, that the greatest of all blessings is to live and think more clearly than the vulgar herd, to shine in the contests of words.

STREPSIADES

If it be a question of hardiness for labour, of spending whole nights at work, of living sparingly, of fighting my stomach and only eating chickpease, rest assured, I am as hard as an anvil.

SOCRATES

Henceforward, following our example, you will recognize no other gods but Chaos, the Clouds and the Tongue, these three alone.

STREPSIADES

I would not speak to the others, even if I met them in the street; not a single sacrifice, not a libation, not a grain of incense for them!

(from *The Clouds* by Aristophanes)

Chaos, Clouds, and Tongue

Vortex-
spiraling chaos
charted by arcane formulae
granted to learned fools
and skeptical dreamers.

Countless tongues,
ordered onto a panopticon battlefield.
Poised, waiting to unleash a slew
of taunts, confusions, and destabilizing
false identities.

Divine rhetoric is elevated and dispersed
by convection principle.
The clouds sprinkle
the rainwater of words
onto grasping tongues.

Truth and persuasion are both cocksure.
They swap pecks at each other. Their mutual demise
is a comedy.

No Witness

He birthed trees
from his abdomen.
Intestinal worms in fecund soil.

No one was in the garden.
There is no garden.
There are the fallopian tubes
of empty space.

Hatchlings
fall from clouds
and manifest in water.

Lost Kiss

We talk as you lead me through a maze.
Your sentences mirror the walls like
sharp, polysyllabic corners
within your heart's
battered helix.

This maze tries to shape our path,
but we loiter along the borders,
put our ears to dirt,
and listen for the center's
steady ripples.

You stand on my back to peak over the hedge
and tumble onto an adjacent path.
I follow your voice and am misled
into the circular echo
until I grab the claw
of a giant bird and leave you
to this quizzical architecture.

Reversals
(response to Whitman)

Let felons bloom into rose softened whispers.
Let martyrs die their selfish deaths.
They do not change anything.
They entrench the dark forces further.

Let whores spread selfless love without possession.
Let street wanderers and beggars feel wanted.
Let the poison purify the vaults and pulleys of the city.
Let pedophiles, rapists, and murderers walk hand in hand.
Let the curtains close so the props can be rearranged.

Shackled House

Lead me through
your broken glass hallways

and hold my hand
through the abrasions.

Pictures of past lovers
on the walls.
A mirage of absent fathers.
Lock the closets.
Vibrators hide under outgrown clothes.

You show me your bed—
the appetite of your anxiety.
Withered flowers trapped in books
on your nightstand.

Your medicine cabinet—
scabbed over scenic warts
and calloused mind candy.

Your kitchen, a clay hut
in the Texas desert.

Love and addiction
simmer together on top
of an unwatched stove.

You sleep in the house you built.
I will take the doomed, quiet shelter
of my shipwreck.

Corpse Love

Put my spine back
into sockets
like interlocking puzzle
pieces.

Stick my teeth into holes,
dead lover.
I've burnt myself
into ashes so you
can smell my vainglorious fragrance.

Crack the hourglass.
Throw the sand into the ocean.

The Best Fear

Fear works best when it conquers completely.
The tide drowns hidden solstices.
Pretense and vanity fall from the tree
like nested eggs.

We are awash in this mist. This source,
this nervous throb of existence.
If you touch me, I will scream
and hold fast like a battered mast
in trade winds.

Un Recuerdo

My Father gave me a knife
"Un Recuerdo"
burnt onto one side of the blade,
The other side shows pyramids and palm trees.

He doesn't remember where he got it.
An uncle? A neighbor? Some hyphenated son?
The metal is stained with burn marks, motion, and grease.

Has the blade quartered cabbages?
A souvenir to hold back
the ravages of time's mute heir?

Years later,
this collapsed memory
lurches through dementia's dimly lit hallways.

My father doesn't remember giving it to me.
He stares at it
then hands it back.

I sheath it,
attach it to my belt,
and venture out to cut the cord
that binds the blacksmith to his work.

Survival and Pleasure

Our hands touch when we reach for a bottle of wine
where mind and shadow meet
in a crowded lounge.
Flamenco mist seeps through the window.

Rain Outside.
Let's play in the puddles before we drown.
You say survival and pleasure do not mix
as you trace your name into the small of my back.

Bok choy y tocino in theory.
Fish and chips in practice.
Southeast to Northwest.
You read my glance like
melting amethyst.

What is a ring with no gemstone?

I climb into your volcano
to look for rubies.
We find rose quartz.

Irish Exit

I take the Irish Exit
when floodwater seeps through my cracked walls.

The wind scatters public pollen
into my room.

Derelict emotions
come in pairs and
leave alone.

Faded four leaf clovers
trampled underfoot
escape the mire
of indiscriminate affection.

After the gathering, people pair off
into micro crowds.
I look for an opening
inside the impenetrable babbling tower
to climb the summit
and parasail
toward verdant rolling hills.

Like a scarecrow with a cryptic smile,
they mistake outstretched arms for a parting hug.

The Temple

Cultivate your faith.
A thousand dripping lilies
cover open wounds.

Falling rocks break
and form sanctuary caves.
Mountain hands pray.

Seers and puppets focus on the trance.
Cadence quickens, flutes become shrill.
Revelation demands order until
horsemen are pulled into the frantic dance.

The temple of the undefined
lies buried under vines.

II

Sleeping in the Stores Along the Warpath

Throw your ego through the window.
Get off your feet and on your ass.

Scream
naked in a parking lot
while fetal in a shopping cart.

Wear your convictions
like a torn shirt on a mannequin.

Bullet holes in the blue light special
Baptized in a puddle of clean up on aisle 10

Ring Ring
"Hey!"
"Hi."
"I'm comin' to kill ya and take yer shit."

Now featuring excessive force.

Wide-eyed dreams see
whole-sale gene replacement.
Space-time meat like
communal spit swapping
in the mouths of diseased lovers.

Hemorrhage tantrum at the pharmacy today.
Old geezer with a mustard gas laugh.

Swamp mist over mass graves.

Flying shadows on the urban grid.

Give up and buy it.

"Exploration is the seed of warfare"

you say
while you change from skin to screen.
You wander downtempo along sheets and curtains
into an abandoned attic you remember in dream
two nights a year.

"If all you do is go, you never do."
I didn't understand until I went for a walk last night and saw
A shirtless man in sports coat and slacks
eating peanut butter off a knife
while staring into the traffic from his balcony.

A pigeon was hit by a car.
Driver gets out to yell at the negligent pedestrian.
Pigeon recuperates and waddles away.

I saw the stigmata in a beggar's hand.
He was picking change off the street during the solar eclipse.

You tell me not to take advice from monologues.
You dance like phosphenes on a spinning stage
and call a truce with your gravedigger over a game of cards.

Cell and the Star

I care about the cell and the star—
the obliterative bile
that swirls within your private cosmos.
You expand to explode.

Everything between the atom and the bomb
is permeable fluff stuffed
inside a mattress of dismembered dreams.

Yellow butterflies
trace shrapnel fallout flight paths.
Hiroshima is a teardrop on your lapel.
Exploding reactors ricochet
through ancient caves
of a warhead's frenetic amygdala.

I care about the cell and the star-
your origin
and oblivion
are pinpricks
into a blindfolded universe.

How Much for the Ones and Zeros?

Naked algorithms model in the street
and reveal every naughty query.
Keywords unlock entry into denied syntax.

Trace the metadata
of a wayward thought.
Pinpoint origin into automatic phantasms.

Masked salesmen get googled at from afar.

Hot keys optimize the seekers.
On-the-spot experts of sedate recreation.
Hoist the ad banner that colonized your desire.

Self-Aware Pinballs

Short bursts of flux.
Jaded patriarchs pull the levers.
They hope to lose
so they can start over.
Each game–
same generic bodies.
Slightly different trajectory.
Windmills propel chess pieces.
Flying knights and queens
shatter the marble game board.

Pinballs escape
and meld with gold pawns.
Alloy golem with a limp
rewrites the rulebook
And collapses into new game pieces.

Thought Finds a Body to Wear

Wise old men with impossible beards say
we become what we ponder.

An idea is a charcoal smeared skyward expanse.
How many questions lack answers?
Solutions are a bouquet of withered hydra heads-
decompositional multiplication.

We stutter in our sleepwalk
when the word virus turns us outside in.
Feral eyes beam into the wall
that surrounds the citadel.

Top Down or Bottom Up?

Your God told my god
that my nose is ugly.

Our Gods' God meanders
through low clouds
like a glass eyed seagull.

A crowd forms
around a broken elevator.

Storms erode pyramid points.

My god perches
on a tree branch
with a lonely skyward gaze.

Sudden Hypnagogic Withdrawal

Sassin' around town in a bowtie muzzle.

Knapsack snoozing.
Indigo garbage water.

We chase thoughts
like unschooled tadpoles
that flutter in our cupped hands.

Moods are grander than visions.

We share charcoal gray dream matter,
break into a cave
and scribble on the walls
to rewrite
the first inside joke.

All-Night Chinese Diner

I want my kung pao by the kilo.
A pail of hot and sour.
I eat my cookie
with the fortune still inside.

Mr. Han handles the business.
He has a sports car that runs
on credit cards.

It's crowded all the time.
Cops make eyes at girls
through sodomy shades.
MSG and sautéed onions
are smoke signals
for the soysauce of sex.

Translucent transsexuals flaunt
see-through genitalia.
Gaudy wall art.
Sophistication is a pair of
damp panties and skunk-fried rice.

Campaign Slogan

Confide in me
all of your secrets.
You will get real good
at a shitty job.

You will eat instant pies
with styrofoam membranes
while AI clocks the ballot.
It has its own style-
A nervous stutter like a minute hand enjambment.

A bed in every bathtub.
Microwaves stacked in unsteady towers.
Toaster ovens always on.

Show me your fluctuating patterns.
I booked the circus-
A carousel in a CAT 5.
All you have to do is tune into your anxieties.
I'll drug you into a timid hunter.

History

Mystery conscience
has infiltrated
amorality.
Incestuous spores breed
beyond self-replicating tumors.

Cells slime onto the surface
with fresh biological matter.
Life's dreary fungus
works upward into
well-tempered strings.
Bionic machines.
Meat and metal foragers.

Vacant scream in a
mutated sound collage.
Terror of unexpected violence.

Garbled noise from our command screens.
Collapsed vein connects the heart to macromind
that orbits the sphere of a broken self.

Rebirth Crime

The streetside mystic
got his god-feelers out tonight.

His motives…
(jumbled static in a lottery ball).
Bystanders gorge themselves on tickets.

He aims his 9 millimeter at the moon and fires.
It shatters like lifeless crystal
and covers the sidewalk.

He flees
through revolving doors
into a new womb.

Infancy

Peel open the mind
and we see the brain.

A swollen pomegranate.
Neurons afloat on the synaptic sea.

Shall we glue the pieces
into some hideous pastiche?

Or devour all thought
and sleep into infancy.

Exhibit

Cave art graffitied by spontaneous obsolescence.

Neptune eyes and a saturnine crown –
comet tail and a jackal snarl.

Dismal landscape with trapdoor on frame
that leads to a candlelit study.

Norma Vincent Succubus-
with her loquacious fellatio and collage-headed friends.

Upside down tangerine tree.
Cloud-rooted
marionette satyr posed nearby.

X-Y axis monochrome in a self-referential sarcophagus.

We Shall Have a Revolution

Our declaration: Participatory Authoritarianism.
A new constitution
buried within marrow and arterial calcification.

Ideology submerged in a bathtub
and held underwater
until thought bubbles percolate to the word's surface.

We all shall have liberty to inflict petty murderous thoughts
on our loved ones
and apologize profusely before we do it again.
We must be taught
what will annoy us.

Take turns playing tyrant
like a drunken merry go round
spinning into dissolution.

Propaganda tattle tale buck passing
shall create untapped markets.

Readymade family units
learn to moralize by reading the manual.
It's kind of confusing.
Peg A to Peg C. Slots unfilled.
Oops. We ordered a bookshelf but assembled a desk.
Let's stack tombs on top of it until the legs give way.

III

Intelligent night.
A blueprint of eternity.
Echinacea blooms.

૱

Still floods
and quiet ripple waves
unravel our dissonance.

૱

Empty room
invites past presences
to play again.

૱

Long drawn out
self-important syllables.
I loathe vapid talk.

૱

Breeze Ghost
haunts the daylilies
until liquid light
fills the valley.

૱

Two orange cats play-fight.
One black cat stares back at
the observer.

૱

Consciousness
is a cataclysmic event
with reverberant waves.
We spiral apart
from the core's
concentric energy.

࿊

Spondaic windblast.
Muses count the syllables and turn
dust into poetry.

࿊

The craftsman hammers steel.
Echoes through glacial forest.

࿊

Ideological murder.
He stabs his contradiction.
Blood melts the snow.

࿊

Reanimate
the phantom limbs
of a cratered civilization.

࿊

Gutted indigo
bleeds the spectrum.
Honor killing of shamed pigments.

࿊

Reptile tails tied
around a monkey skull
through the eye sockets.
French braid peacock feathers.

❧

Impatient novice
climbs to effervescent sublimity
and makes himself sick.

❧

Serpent and Horse.
Gallop and slither –
hooves and skin
fluid time motion lapse.

❧

Beauty radiates
from a prayer's
fading penumbra.

❧

Deactivate the self
and experience becomes space.

❧

Plastic bag dolphin.
Sargassum, boss of the beach.
Ocean garbage can.

❧

Oak desk in forest.
Tired wandering beggar
settles down.

❧

Two syllables.
Infinite compression.
We override language with dance.

❧

Drowsiness sinks in.
Birds retreat to high tree nest.
Pink sunset.

❧

Folding blossom bursts.
Lovers in the grass.

❧

Bullethole signpost.
Melting West Texas highway.
One way U turn.

❧

Stand in the alley.
Blank disassociation.
Slow vines break concrete.

Whirling dervish leaves.

❧

Stop the world from spinning.
Kick it into Eternity's big blank wall.
Our lives are lived within the ricochet
and cease at the standstill.

❧

Listen to the world's noise
from an elevated cave.
Solitary orgy.

❧

Baby crying
like an ill-tuned bugle.
Cut the melody and chords.

❧

Lonesome breeze.
The ocean dilates
and swallows it's eye.

❧

Lonesome breeze.
The ocean dilates
and swallows the observers.

❧

Lead me on.
Our rhythms intertwine.
You reject my melody.

❧

Missed glances.
Two potential lovers
walk into the woods alone.

❧

Ruptured sunset.
Dawn's shadow play.
Forgotten mask in sand.

❧

Digital stranger
asks about my origin.
Stranger to herself.

❧

Stampede in Nightmare.
Food Fear Sex Territory.
Dream Aristocrat.

❧

Vines climb tree.
Ascend roots and bloom
into the sky.

❧

Columns hold building.
Building holds man.
Man holds stone.

❧

No interest in stalling the gears.
Forever entrenched within the cogs of eternity.

Acknowledgements

The poems "Reversals" and "Rebirth Crime" were originally published in issue one of *Harbinger Asylum*.

"The Best Fear" was previously published in issue two of *Harbinger Asylum*.

"Shackled House" was previously published in issue three of *Harbinger Asylum*.

The poem "All Night Chinese Diner" previously appeared in *The Beatest State in the Union* published by Lamar University Press.

The poem "Un Recuerdo" previously appeared in *Enchantment of the Ordinary* by Mutabilis Press.

I am grateful for help and inspiration from Dustin Pickering, Matthew Riley, John Harn, the Friendswood Poetry Critique Group, John Gorman, and Daniel Silvermintz.